True Grit

Southern Cooking and Canning

Recipe Book

A cookbook for your home, featuring easy to follow recipes for both cooking from scratch and food preservation.

Index

Appetizers & Sides

Fried Green Tomatoes

Fried green tomatoes is not only a good movie, but an excellent appetizer! It is a staple in southern cooking, everyone has their own tips, tricks and recipes. I thought I would share mine with you.

You will need:

3-4 Firm Green Tomatoes

AP Flour

½ cup buttermilk

Cooking Oil

Self-Rising

Corn Meal

Cut your green tomatoes into slices or chunks. Add buttermilk to tomatoes, combine, make sure all tomatoes are coated with buttermilk. Add enough cornmeal to have a good coating on tomatoes. Add approx. ½ cup AP flour, combine again. Add to hot oil, fry until golden brown.

Cheeseburger Soup

You will need:

1 lb. hamburger

1 can cheddar cheese soup.

onions and any other veggies of your choice

1 cup shredded cheddar cheese

½ cup milk potatoes

1 qt chicken broth

First brown hamburger, sauté onions and any other veggies in butter. Cube potatoes and add to hamburger. Pour chicken broth into hamburger/ potato mixture, simmer until potatoes are tender. Add cheddar cheese soup and shredded cheese, stir until melted. In a separate pan make a roux with flour and butter, add to soup mixture, simmer until soup is the thickness of your choice. Turn heat on low, add milk, cooked veggies and salt/pepper to taste. Then enjoy!

Mama's Vegetable Meat Soup

2 quarts of tomato juice

*optional*crushed red pepper flakes.

1 lb. meat of your choice

Cooked mixed vegetables.

Cook meat until done, you can use beef, pork, chicken or a mixture. Add tomato juice to large stock pot. Add meat, add mixed vegetable (do not drain), salt and pepper to taste, 1 tbsp crushed red pepper flakes. Stir together, let simmer for at least 30 minutes so all flavors can combine. Serve with grilled cheese, freeze leftovers for a quick meal on a rainy day!

Sweet Acorn Squash

1 acorn squash brown sugar

½ stick of butter.

¼ cup water

cinnamon

Preheat oven to 350 degrees. Cut acorn squash in half. Clean out seeds. Melt butter and paint flesh of acorn squash. Sprinkle with cinnamon and brown sugar. Place on baking sheet. Pour ¼ cup water in bottom of baking sheet. Cover with aluminum foil, cook for 50 minutes. Remove cover, bake for an additional 10 minutes. Serve warm.

Buttermilk Mac and Cheese

Macaroni Noodles

4 cups buttermilk

½ stick butter.

2 eggs, beaten.

8 oz shredded cheese

Preheat oven to 350 degrees. Cook noodles until al dente. In a separate pan add butter, buttermilk and cheese, cook until everything is melted and combined. Add eggs. Add noodles to 8x8 pan. Pour cheese sauce over noodles. Cook in oven for 45-60 minutes, until sauce has thickened. Let cool, serve and enjoy!

Easy Made from Scratch Noodles

I remember the first time I made noodles. I was amazed at the simplicity of the process! Y'all the hands-on time for this is about 15 minutes and the taste is out of this world. Everyone's tastes are a little different for me I like to add just a tad extra salt than this recipe calls for. Experiment and keep trying until you get the exact taste you are looking for!

2 cups all-purpose flour

1 Tbsp Salt

3 eggs

Mix the dry ingredients, make a pond in the middle, add the eggs, beat the eggs and slowly pull in flour, you'll eventually have a slightly crumbly dough Lay on a floured surface and knead for 8 min (If the dough is still crumbly add a little water) Let sit for 45 min, then roll dough ball out as flat as you can get it Use pizza cutter to cut out noodles, hang on a clothes hanger to dry (cont.)

or cook them to al dente If drying for shelf storage dry for at least 24 hours or until there is no give in the noodles, they should be shelf stable in airtight container for about 6 months!

Sweet Potato Cobbler

2-4 sweet potatoes baked and peeled.

1 cup brown sugar

½ stick butter.

2 containers of crescent rolls

Cinnamon

½ cup white sugar

Preheat oven to 375 degrees. Grease 8x8 pan Unroll 1 package of crescents, place in bottom of pan. Slice cooked/peeled sweet potatoes and place on top of dough. In separate microwavable bowl add butter, white sugar, brown sugar and cinnamon, microwave until butter is melted. Stir until combined, pour mixture over potatoes being sure all are covered. Unroll half of 2nd package of crescents, place on top until all potatoes are covered, pinch seams and edges together. Cook in preheated oven for approx. 20 min or until dough is golden brown. *optional sprinkle a little extra brown sugar and cinnamon on top Slice and serve as a side dish or dessert!

Fried Pickles

1 pint jar of dill pickles

2 cups flour

1 tsp cayenne pepper

1 tsp cumin

1 Tbsp old bay

1 tsp garlic

1 egg and splash of milk for wash

Lay your pickles out on a paper towel to dry. Heat oil in deep fryer or deep pot, you need enough cooking oil to cover the pickles. In a gallon size plastic bag, mix flour, spices, salt and pepper. Drop the pickles into bag, shake until all are coated. Whisk egg and milk together and dredge flour covered pickles through the egg wash. Return pickles to flour. Shake again. Place pickles in hot oil and fry for 1-2 minutes per side or until golden brown. A good dipping sauce, is cayenne pepper powder, mixed with ranch!

Main Dishes

Pizza Dough

2¼ tsp active dry yeast or 1 packet

2½ cups bread flour

2 Tbsp olive oil

1 tsp sugar

1 tsp salt

1 cup warm water

Dissolve yeast and sugar into 1 cup warm water, until creamy, let sit approx. 10 minutes. Stir in flour, salt and oil. Mix until smooth, you may add a small amount of additional warm water if dough is too dry. Let rest for 5 minutes. Dough can be frozen or refrigerated. When ready to make pizza, turn dough out onto lightly floured surface and pat or roll into a circle. Transfer to lightly greased pizza pan dusted with cornmeal.

Pizza/Marinara Sauce

2 Tbsp olive oil

½ tsp dried oregano (optional)

1 clove garlic, minced. (optional)

black pepper to taste for thickening.

1 qt canned tomatoes

Pinch of crushed red peppers

½ Tbsp sugar

1 tsp dried basil

½ cup cornstarch,

¾ tsp salt

Add 2 tbsp. olive oil to sauce pot, heat over med high, add minced garlic. Cook garlic until soft and aromatic. Add remaining ingredients. Bring to boil, reduce to simmer for 15-30 min, until sauce is as thick as you would like. This freezes well in freezer bags or freezer safe containers after it has cooled.

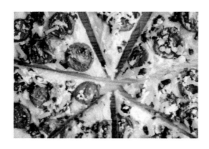

Homemade Pizza

Pizza dough

½ lb. ground sausage

pizza sauce

cooked bacon, chopped.

1 pkg pepperoni's

1½ cup shredded cheese

Preheat oven to 450 degrees. Roll out pizza dough into a large circle. Fold edges to make crust and place onto a greased or dusted pizza pan (see Made from Scratch Pizza Dough). Apply pizza sauce liberally (see Pizza sauce). Apply ¾ cup shredded cheese. Then apply toppings, the above are just a guide, apply whatever toppings you would like. Then apply remaining ¾ cup shredded cheese onto toppings. Place in oven, cook for 15-20 minutes or until crust is golden brown. Paint crust with melted butter, let cool 5 minutes and enjoy!

Chicken Stew

6 lbs. chicken

6 qt boiling water (for chicken)

1 stick of butter

4-6 cups milk

1-2 cups flour

Salt and pepper to taste.

Place chicken in a large pot and cover with water, cook until you can easily pull meat apart. Remove chicken from broth and let cool. Bring broth to a boil, add the stick of butter. Mix milk and flour in a bowl, add it to the broth. Add salt and pepper to taste. Boil until soup mixture is as thick as you would like, then add in chicken.

Chocolate Chip Pancakes

2 cups bisquick   Chocolate Chips

1 Tbsp honey   2 eggs

1 cup of buttermilk

Combine all ingredients, butter a skillet. Fry ½ cup batter at a time, flip when you start seeing bubbles on edges of pancake. Enjoy with syrup!

Chicken Noodle Soup

1-2 cups shredded cooked chicken.

2 cups milk

Egg noodles

1-2 cups chicken broth

Mixed vegetables (cooked) of your choice

1 stick of butter

Melt butter, chicken, and broth together Add milk, add veggies. Bring to simmer, add noodles Cook, occasionally stirring, until noodles are al dente Easy as that! Hope you enjoy!

Taco Meat

2-3 cups shredded meat of your choice.

½ block cream cheese

1 cup shredded cheese

taco sauce

Mix all ingredients, heat until cheese is melted and combined. Serve with your favorite taco night choice!

Chicken Pie

1 can cream of chicken.

1 cup milk-halved

1 can mixed vegetables.

1 cup cooked, cubed chicken.

1 egg

1 cup biscuit mix

Heat oven to 400 degrees. Combine cream of chicken, ½ cup milk, veggies-drained, and chicken into deep baking dish. In a separate bowl combine biscuit mix, ½ cup milk, egg. Spread batter over top of chicken mixture (batter will be thin). Bake 20-25 minutes or until topping is golden brown. Paint the top with butter last 5 minutes of cooking.

Pulled Pork

Put whatever rub you would like on your pork shoulder.

Place in a pan with approx. 12 oz liquid

You can use chicken broth, beer, water, whatever you would like.

Put in an oven heated to 450° for 30 min.

Cover with foil.

Decrease heat to 300°

Cook until you reach an internal temp of 170°

Then after I pull my pork, I add BBQ sauce. Vacuum seal or place in freezer safe container to freeze.

Breads

Buttermilk Biscuits

Biscuits are one of those things, that once you figure out how to make that perfect fluffy biscuit, you have made the ultimate accomplishment in the kitchen. At least that is the way my family and friends are around here. I worked on making biscuits, experimenting for at least a year before I finally mastered it. Here is my recipe.

2½ cups self-rising flour

1 stick cold butter.

½ Tbsp sugar

1 cup cold buttermilk

Preheat oven to 425 degrees. Mix all dry ingredients. Using a fork or pastry cutter, mash in butter until flour is course, leave no pieces larger than pea sized. Add buttermilk. Stir gently just until all dry ingredients are wet. Flour surface. Roll out dough and cut into circles using cookie cutter or floured cup. Careful not to twist. Place on greased pan. Cook for approx. 18 minutes or until biscuits are golden brown. Paint the tops with melted butter. Let cool and enjoy!

Tips for the Perfect Biscuit

- Use cold butter, straight out of the fridge or freezer, do not let it sit on the counter while you are getting the rest of the ingredients mixed up.
- Mix ingredients until they are just combined, over mixing makes tough biscuits.
- Place biscuits directly into an already heated oven
- To get taller biscuits, add an extra sprinkle of baking powder to dry ingredients and be sure biscuits are touching when placed on the pan.

Hushpuppies

1 cup self-rising cornmeal

¼ cup sugar

1 cup self-rising flour

1¼ cup buttermilk

2 eggs at room temperature

¼ cup oil

¾ cup diced onions.

vegetable oil for frying

Pour oil 3 inches deep in pan, heat to temp of 325 degrees. Combine dry ingredients, then add wet ingredients. Stir until all dry ingredients are moist. Let stand for 10 min for batter to thicken. Drop batter by rounded tablespoons into hot oil, 2-3 minutes each side or until golden brown. Note: To keep warm, place in 200-degree oven until ready to serve.

Pone Bread

2½ cups self-rising flour

½ stick butter.

1½ Tbsp sugar

approx. 1 cup buttermilk

¼ cup lard

Preheat oven to 450 degrees. Mix dry ingredients. Cut in lard and butter with fork or pastry cutter. Add buttermilk, mix until all dry ingredients are moist. Pour in cast iron pan or glass baking dish, cook for 20-30 min or until top is golden brown. Let cool and enjoy any time of day!

Easy Cinnamon Rolls

1 can biscuits cinnamon

2 tbsp melted butter

Brown Sugar

White Sugar

Cinnamon

Icing: 1 cup confectionary sugar

1-2 tbsp milk

Lay biscuits out together in rows of 2, pinch edges together, the roll out flat. Paint the top with melted butter, sprinkle a thin layer of white sugar, sprinkle a layer of brown sugar, then sprinkle cinnamon to taste. Roll into a log, starting with the short side. Using a sharp knife, cut the roll in approximately 1-inch sections. Lay them in your pan, cook at 375 degrees for 15-20 minutes. While they are cooking prepare your icing. In a mixing bowl add confectionary sugar, slowly add milk, combine until the icing is as thick or thin as you'd like. Apply to hot cinnamon rolls and enjoy!

Pie Dough

3 cups AP flour

1 cup cold or frozen lard

1 Tbsp vinegar

cold water

1 Tbsp sugar

1 tsp salt

1 egg

Pour vinegar and egg into mixing cup, combine. Add enough cold water to mixing cup to make ½ cup of liquid. Set aside. Combine flour, sugar, and salt. Add lard and cut into flour until lard pieces  are no larger than a pea. Slowly add liquid while mixing. A soft crumbly dough will form. If dough will not hold together add just a little more cold water. Remove dough from bowl, separate and shape into 2 balls of dough. Cover in plastic wrap and refrigerate for at least 1 hour before cooking. This dough also freezes well in a freezer safe container.

Desserts

Peach Cobbler

1 cup fresh/frozen peaches or 1 can of peaches

1 cup milk

1 cup self-rising flour

½ stick melted butter.

1 cup sugar

If using fresh/frozen peaches, you will also need:

1 cup water

1 cup sugar

Preheat oven to 350 degrees. Combine water, 1 cup sugar, and fresh/ frozen peaches in saucepan, cook until sugar is dissolved. If using canned peaches skip this step. In a mixing bowl combine milk, melted butter, sugar and flour. Pour in a greased 8x8 baking dish for fluffier cobbler, or 9x13 for a "flatter" cobbler. Pour peaches and juice throughout mixture, do not stir. Place in oven and cook for approximately 30-45 minutes or until crust is golden and bubbling. Let cool and enjoy with some vanilla ice cream!

Apple Pie

1½ cups dried apples

cinnamon

Boiling water

ginger

1 /3 cups white sugar

Pie dough

½ cup brown sugar

Preheat oven to 375 degrees. Roll out pie dough, place in pie pan. In a bowl add dried apples, pour just enough boiling water into apples until they are about half covered (not completely covered). Let sit for 5 minutes, add brown sugar, white sugar, cinnamon and ginger, combine. Pour into pie dough, cover with 2nd pie dough, cut holes to vent or cut strips to make latus on top, place in oven, cook for approx. 30 min. Remove from oven, paint crust with butter or egg wash. Cook for an additional 5 minutes or until crust is golden brown. Let cool and enjoy!

Chocolate Cake

1 ¾ cup self-rising flour

1 cup milk

2 cups white sugar
oil

½ cup vegetable

¾ cup cocoa powder

½ tsp vanilla

2 eggs

1 cup hot water

Preheat oven to 375 degrees. Combine dry ingredients first. Add wet ingredients, everything except the water, mix on medium speed for 2 minutes. After mixing, add hot water and combine. Pour into 9"x13" pan, cook approx. 35-45 minutes. Remove from oven, let cool completely and add icing of your choice.

Peanut Butter Delight

2 cups sugar

½ cup milk

2 tsp vanilla

½ cup butter

4 Tbsp cocoa

½ cup peanut butter

2 ½ cup oatmeal

Combine sugar, milk, vanilla, butter, and cocoa, bring mixture to a boil, boil for 2 minutes. Add peanut butter and oatmeal. Stir well, drop by teaspoonfuls onto wax paper and refrigerate. Allow to cool completely, then enjoy!

Brownies

1 cup melted butter.

½ cup cocoa

2 cups all-purpose flour

2 cups sugar

4 eggs

1 Tbsp vanilla

Preheat oven to 350 degrees, grease brownie or cake pan, mix all ingredients until smooth. Cook for approximately 40-50 minutes or until brownies are cook through.

Frosting

¼ cup softened butter

¼ cup milk

¼ cup cocoa

3 cups powdered sugar.

¼ tsp salt

Mix all ingredients until smooth. Apply to top of brownies after they have cooled.

Food
Preservation

Food preservation is one of my many passions, my favorite option being canning our food. There are a million recipes out there and for some one that is new or wanting to get back into canning, it can be overwhelming.

So, I wanted to share with you my favorite tried and true recipes, that even someone who is inexperienced with canning can do.

Before we get started always remember to follow your pressure canners directions for safety. Always sterilize your canning jars, lids, and rings, by boiling in water or using the sanitize option on your dishwasher before beginning your process.

Now let us get started.

Tomato Juice

10 lbs. tomatoes

Canning Salt

Citric Acid or Lemon Juice

Wash tomatoes, core and quarter. Place in pot, bring to simmer, until tomatoes become soft. Strain. Reheat juice to boil, skim film from the top. Bring back to boil. Put hot juice into hot jars, add citric acid or lemon juice (optional helps tomatoes keep their color). Add 1 tsp canning salt per quart or ½ tsp for pints. Water bath for 30 minutes and store. Note: You can use this recipe for as many or as few tomatoes as you would like

Sweet Chow Chow

1 medium cabbage head

4 cups onions

4-5 green tomatoes (4 cups)

4 cups vinegar

3-4 jalapeño peppers (optional)

6 cups sugar

6-7 green bell peppers (4 cups)

2 cups water

4 yellow or red peppers

½ cup salt

Chop all veggies up, place in glass container. Cover with ½ cup salt. Cover and let sit in refrigerator overnight. The next day place mixture in large pot, add all remaining ingredients. Boil for 4-5 minutes. Add hot mixture to hot jars. Place lid and ring. Water bath for 8-10 minutes and store.

Pickled Eggs

1 dozen eggs

3-4 tsp pickling spice

2 cups vinegar

1 tsp minced garlic

1 cup sugar

1 tsp minced onions

2 tbsp salt

Makes 1 qt Peel hard boiled eggs, place in quart size jar. In a saucepan combine vinegar, sugar and salt. Heat until sugar and salt have dissolved. Remove from heat, add pickling spice, garlic and onion. Add hot liquid to eggs in the jar. Apply lid, let sit in refrigerator for at least 2 weeks to give the eggs time to absorb mixture. Good for 3-4 months in the fridge.

Rendering Lard

Pork Leaf Fat

Crockpot

Water

Jars or heat proof container

Put water in crockpot, just enough to cover the bottom. Cube leaf fat, place in crockpot. Cook on low until you have crispy brown cracklings floating in your lard. Ladle into jars or heat proof container using cheese cloth to filter the fine bits out. The cleaner the lard the longer it will last. Apply lid to container, allow to cool. Store in cool dry space, shelf stable for at least 1 year.

Bacon

3-5 lb. pork belly

2.5 Tbsp plain salt

2 tbsp of maple syrup

1 tsp freshly ground black pepper.

3 Tbsp sugar (white or brown or pepper both)

Mix all ingredients together, rub onto pork belly generously, place in a zip lock bag. Refrigerate, flip every day for 7 days. After 7 days place pork belly into oven at 200°, cook until you receive an internal temp of 145°. Remove from oven allow to cool completely, slice then freeze and/or enjoy!

Canning Green Beans

String wash and snap green beans. Fill jars leaving 1 inch of head space. Cover green beans with water, add 1 tsp canning salt to quarts or ½ tsp to pints. Place sanitized lids and rings onto jars. Follow your pressure canners directions for water levels, proper use, etc. Process filled jars at 10lbs of pressure 25 minutes for quarts or 20 minutes for pints.

Pickled Beets

Fresh Beets

1 cup water

2½ cups vinegar

1 cup sugar

3 Tbsp pickling spice

Trim fresh beets, leaving at least 1 inch of root and 1 inch of stem. Place in a large pot of boiling water, placing the biggest beets on the bottom. Boil until beets are fork tender. Remove beets from hot water, place directly into ice water. Let sit until cool enough to handle. Cut off root and stem, peel beets. Skin should peel off easily. In a separate pot add vinegar, pickling spice, water, and sugar. Simmer for 15 minutes. Place beets in sterilized jars, boil lids and rings. Add filtered vinegar mixture to jars, cover beets completely. Add lids and rings. Hot water bath for 30 minutes. After jars have sealed and cooled for 24 hours, remove rings, and store in a cool, dark location.

Dill Pickles

8 lbs cucumbers

¾ cup sugar

½ cup preserving/pickling salt

1 qt vinegar

1 qt water

Dill (fresh or dried)

Fresh garlic

Prepare cucumbers, wash them under cold water, cut off the ends, cut into spears or slices. Combine sugar, salt, vinegar, and water in a large pot, bring mixture to a boil, stirring until sugar is dissolved. Reduce heat and simmer for 15 minutes. Put a piece of dill flowre in the bottom of jar and 1 clove of garlic for pints or 2 cloves for quarts. Pack your cucumbers into jar, put another piece of dill flower on top. Ladle hot pickling liquid over pickles until your ½ inch from top of rim. Put lid and ring on jar. Water bath for 15 minutes. Let jars cool for 24 hours. Remove ring, store in cool, dark place.

Chicken Stock

1 chicken carcass

3 sprigs thyme

4-6 qts water

10 peppercorns

2-3 carrots coarsely chopped.

salt to taste

3 bay leaves (optional)

3 Tbsp ACV

1 onion

Mix all ingredients together (stock is forgiving, the ingredients do not have to be exact), if using apple cider vinegar let sit at least 30 minutes before adding heat. The vinegar starts the breakdown of the bones a little faster. Bring mixture to a simmer, cover and let cook on low to med low for approx. 12-36 hours, the longer you cook it, the more nutrients you will get in your stock. When your stock is done cooking, filter through cheese cloth for a clearer stock. Store in airtight container up to 2 weeks in the fridge or add to sterilized jars and pressure can under 10lbs pressure for 20 minutes and store at room temperature. Add this chicken stock to any of your favorite recipes for an increased depth in flavor!

Canning Tomatoes

Fresh Tomatoes

Canning Salt

Citric Acid or Lemon Juice

Core tomatoes. Blanche tomatoes for approximately 1 minute or until skin becomes loose. Remove from boiling water and place directly into cold water. Once tomatoes are cool enough to handle, peel off tomato skin. Quarter large tomatoes leave small tomatoes whole. Place in a sterilized jar, fill to 1" of headspace. Add citric acid or lemon juice and canning salt, 1 tsp for quart, ½ tsp for pint. Take a wooden spoon handle and go around the inside rim of the jar/tomatoes to remove any air bubble. Wipe rim apply sterilized lids and rings. Tomatoes can be canned using water bath or pressure canning method.

Pressure canner: Process under 10lbs. of pressure 25 minutes for pints, 40 minutes for quarts.

Hot water bath: 90 minutes for quarts and/or pints.

Canning Potatoes

Potatoes

Canning Salt

Water

Wash potatoes thoroughly, peel potatoes (you can skip this step as long as your peeling is extremely clean), place in clean sterilized jar. Small potatoes can be left whole or large potatoes can be cut into smaller pieces. Place lid and ring on jar. Pressure can for 40 minutes under 10lbs of pressure. Let cool for 24 hours, remove ring, store in cool, dark place.

Due to the starchiness of potatoes, the water will occasionally be cloudy inside the jar. Always be sure to discard the potato water and rinse potatoes well, before cooking.

Apple Preserves

6 cups of sliced, cored, peeled apples.

1 cup water

1 Tbsp lemon juice

1 package of fruit pectin

4 cups granulated sugar.

1 tsp ground
cinnamon

Combine apples,
water, and lemon
juice. Bring to
boil over high
heat. Reduce heat, cover and gently boil for 10
minutes, stirring occasionally. Remove from heat,
add pectin, stir until completely combined. Return
to high heat, bring to a boil, stir constantly, add
cinnamon. Boil for 1 minute. Remove from heat,
skim foam from top. Ladle hot liquid into hot jars,
leaving ¼ in headspace. Water bath for 10
minutes, let jars cool for 24 hours, remove rings.
Store in a cool dry place.

Preserving Fresh Corn

To freeze: shuck corn, take dry corn and wrap with cling wrap, twisting up the loose ends, place in a freezer bag. Our corn is usually still good for up to a year in the freezer before getting mushy!

To can: shuck corn, wash corn, cut corn off the cob, scraping up the cob after you have cut the corn off to get the juice out of the cob, fill sanitized jars up to the first ring you come to, fill with hot water enough to cover corn, add 1/2 tsp canning salt for pints and 1 tsp for quarts, boil lids, cleanse rims, place lids and rings on, pressure can under 10lbs pressure pints 55 minutes, quarts 85 minutes!

The True Grit Communtiy

Crockpot Buffalo Chicken Dip

By: Lisa Rogers

2 cooked chicken breasts shredded.

½ cup buffalo sauce

½ cup ranch dressing

8 oz cream cheese

Tortilla chips for dipping

¾ cup shredded cheddar cheese

Mix all ingredients together in crockpot, cook on low until melted. Stir and serve with tortilla chips.

Chicken and Dumplings

In loving memory of all the Moorefield family women

1 chicken (2-3 lbs.) cooked and deboned

½ stick margarine.

2 cups self-rising flour

at least 1 qt broth

1 /3 cup shortening.

1½ cups milk buttermilk

Debone chicken and strain broth. Place back into pot (deep) with milk, margarine, salt, and pepper to taste. Sift flour and mix in shortening. Add buttermilk gradually, beating constantly until you have a shiny batter. The more you beat, the fluffier the dumpling. Drop by spoonful's into boiling chicken mixture. DO NOT STIR! Cover and cook. Yummy!

Cowboy Beans

By: Lisa Rogers

½ lb. bacon

1 can baby lima beans

1 lb. ground beef

1 large onion

¼ cup diced green peppers.

½ tsp dry mustard

1 can pork 'n beans

1 can red kidney beans

1 can great northern beans

¼ cup molasses or maple syrup

½ tsp pepper

1 can butter beans.

1 jar BBQ sauce

¼ cup brown sugar

Cut bacon into ¼" bits, brown in a large skillet. Remove bacon from rendered fat and set aside. In the bacon grease, sauté the onion and pepper until tender. Add the ground meat and brown lightly. Put the meats into the bottom of a crockpot. Add the Pork 'n beans with the liquid. Drain most of the juice off of the remaining cans of beans and add them with the remaining ingredients to the crockpot. Cook on low for 4-6 hours.

Loaded Potato and Buffalo Chicken Casserole

By: Caitlin Sparks

2 lb. boneless chicken breasts cubed.

1 Tbsp Paprika

2 Tbsp garlic powder

8-10 medium potatoes cut into ½" cubes.

6 Tbsp hot sauce Topping

1 /3 cup olive oil

2 cups fiesta blend cheese

1½ tsp salt

1 cup crumbled bacon

1 Tbsp black pepper

1 cup diced green onion.

Preheat oven to 500 degrees. Spray 9 x 13 baking dish with cooking spray. (Continued)

In a large bowl, mix olive oil, salt, pepper, paprika, garlic powder, and hot sauce. Add cubed potatoes and stir to coat. Carefully scoop potatoes into prepared baking dish. Leave behind as much of the hot sauce mixture as possible. Bake potatoes for 45-50 minutes, stirring every 10 - 15 minutes, until cooked through, crispy and brown on the outside. While the potatoes are cooking, add cubed chicken to hot sauce mixture, stir to coat. Once potatoes are fully cooked, remove from oven, decrease oven temp to 400 degrees. Top the cooked potatoes with raw marinated chicken. In a separate bowl mix together fiesta blend cheese, bacon, and onion. Top raw chicken with mixture. Return casserole to oven. Bake for 15 minutes or until chicken is cooked through and the topping is bubbly and delicious. Serve with extra hot sauce and/or ranch dressing.

Banana Pudding

By: Tammie Lawson

3 cups milk	vanilla
1¼ cup granulated sugar	wafers
½ cup flour	3 eggs, separated.
pinch of salt	Bananas

Combine egg yolks, sugar, flour and milk in top of double boiler. Cook and stir until slightly thickened. Remove from heat and stir in vanilla. Place layer of vanilla wafers in bottom of 9"x13" glass baking dish, place layer of sliced bananas on top of wafers, place layer of sauce on top of bananas. Continue alternating layers of wafers, bananas and sauce until dish is full, ending with layer of vanilla wafers. Beat egg whites with pinch of salt until egg whites begin to hold soft peaks. Gradually add 4 tablespoons of sugar and continue beating until egg whites are stiff. Spread on pudding and bake at 400 degrees until slightly browned.

Lemon Meringue Pie

By: Tammie Lawson

1 (15 oz) can sweetened condensed milk.

½ cup lemon juice

2-3 egg yolks

Beat egg yolks and add to milk. Add lemon juice and mix well. Make crust with vanilla wafers in pie plate or use a graham cracker crust. Pour mix into crust. Top with meringue and brown or use a whipped topping.

Margaret's Egg White Topping

In Loving Memory of Margaret Priddy

2 tbsp sugar per egg white   egg whites

Beat egg white(s) until creamy, then add sugar. Beat again until stiff. Beat again until stiff, but not dry. Put on pudding. Bake at 350 degrees until brown.

Margaret's Chocolate Pudding

In Loving Memory of Margaret Priddy

4 egg yolks

1 stick margarine

2 cups sugar

4 cups milk

½ cup flour

1 tsp vanilla

2 tbsp cocoa

Mix all ingredients together except margarine, milk and vanilla. Then add milk. Then add vanilla. Put 1 stick margarine in a double boiler and let melt. Then add all other ingredients. Let cook until thick. Put in glass 9x13 dish. Cover with egg white topping (see Margaret's Egg White Topping).

Red Velvet Cake
(Old Fashioned Recipe)

By: Wanda East

1½ cups sugar

1 cup buttermilk

2 eggs

1 tsp baking soda

2½ cups self-rising flour

1 cup of oil

1 tsp vinegar

1 tsp vanilla

Mix all ingredients. Pour into 3 greased and dusted round cake pans. Bake at 350 for 30 minutes-check at 25 minutes. (see old fashioned red velvet cake icing for next step)

Old Fashioned Red Velvet Cake Icing

By: Wanda East

8 oz softened cream cheese

3½ cups of powdered sugar

1 stick softened butter.

1 cup finely chopped pecans

1 tsp vanilla (optional)

Mix all ingredients and spread on each cake layer and on the sides of cake. This recipe may be doubled for extra icing.

Sweet Potato Delight

By: Twila Williams

1 sleeve crushed Ritz crackers   1 egg

¾ cup sugar   1 tsp vanilla

1 stick Melted butter.

8 oz cool whip

½ stick melted butter.

8 oz cream cheese

¾ cup sugar

crushed pecans

1 large can sweet potatoes, mashed.

For the crust: combine Ritz crackers, 1 stick melted butter. Mash into bottom of dish, cook on 350 degrees for 10 minutes. Next combine cool whip, cream cheese, and ¾ cup sugar. Place on top of cooked crust. Then mix sweet potatoes, ¾ cup sugar, 1 egg, ½ stick melted butter, vanilla together in microwave safe bowl. Microwave for 3 minutes. Layer on top of cool whip mixture. Top with crushed pecans.

Barbequed Hot Dogs

By: Kathy Young

32 oz bottle of ketchup

32 oz grape jelly

2 packs of Ball Park beef hotdogs

Put ketchup and jelly in a crockpot. Mix well and melt all grape jelly. Cut hot dogs into 1/6-inch slices and pour into mixture. Let cook until hot dogs have increased in size.

Chunky Pickles

By: Kathy Young

2 gal. cucumbers cut in cubes 1 inch long.

1 pint salt cover with boiling water, for 1 week, stir each day.

Drain: Add 2 heaping Tbsp alum. Cover with boiling water, stand 24 hours.

Mix: 8 pints sugar, 2 quarts vinegar, ½ box pickling spice (tied in cloth), 2 Tbsp mustard seed, 1 tsp turmeric. Bring to boil daily for 3 days. On the 3rd day, can your pickles.

Buttermilk Pancakes

By: Kathy Young

2 cups self-rising flour

2 Tbsp sugar

¼ tsp baking soda

2 eggs

1 ½ cup buttermilk

¼ cup melted shortening or cooking oil

Sift all dry ingredients together. Beat eggs slightly. Stir in buttermilk. Add shortening, then add the dry ingredients. Beat until smooth. Cook on hot griddle or in heavy frying pan, which has been greased.

Frozen Corn

By: Kathy Young

8 cups corn

½ cup sugar

1 tsp salt

2 cups water

Mix ingredients and bring to a boil for 10 minutes. Cool and put into freezer bags or freezer safe container.

Turkey Pot Pie

By: Kathy Young

1 ½ cups frozen peas and carrots, thawed.

5 Tbsp butter

5 Tbsp all-purpose flour

¼ cup chopped onion.

½ tsp salt

¼ tsp pepper

1 ¾ cups turkey or chicken broth

2/3 cup milk

2 ½ to 3 cups diced cooked turkey or chicken.

Pastry for 9-inch, 2 crust pie, prepared or purchased.

Drain peas and carrots; set aside. Heat butter in 2-quart saucepan over low heat until melted. Stir in flour, onion, salt and pepper. Cook, stirring constantly, until mixture is bubbly; remove from heat then stir in broth and milk. Place back on heat; heat to boiling, stirring constantly. Boil and stir 1 minute. Stir in turkey and vegetables.(Cont.)

Prepare pastry. Roll 2/3 of the pastry into a 13-inch square; ease into ungreased 9-inch square pan. Pour turkey mixture into the pastry-lined pan. Roll remaining pastry into 11-inch square; cut out designs with small cookie cutter. Place square over filling; turn edges under and crimp. Bake in 425-degree oven until golden brown, about 35 minutes.

Serves 6.

Pound Cake

By: Kathy Young

1 cup of butter	1 cup milk
½ cup shortening	¼ tsp salt.
3 cups sugar	2 tsp lemon extract
6 eggs	½ tsp baking powder
3 cups of plain flour (no cake flour)	

Cream butter and shortening, add sugar and cream well. Add eggs one at a time, beat hard after each addition. Add sifted ingredients gradually with milk and continue beating. Add lemon extract and pour into a greased flour tube pan. Bake 1 hour and 15 minutes at 325 degrees.

Pound Cake Icing

1 tsp vanilla 1 8oz cream cheese

1 box confectionary sugar 1 stick margarine

1 cup of pecans

Mix all ingredients together and ice the cake!

Apple Nut Pound Cake

By: Kathy Young

3 large apples or 4 medium apples equal to 3 cups yellow delicious apples diced.

3 cups self-rising flour

2 cups granulated sugar.

1 1/3 cups Crisco

3 eggs

1 cup chopped pecans or black walnuts.

¾ cup bakers' coconut

1 ½ tsp vanilla

Mix sugar and oil. Add eggs, flour, mix good, add vanilla and apples. Add nuts and coconut, combine well. Pour into greased and floured pan or tube pan. Bake in 350-degree oven, in long pan for 1 hour, tube pan 1 ½ hours.

Apple Pie

By: Kathy Young

¾ cup white sugar

1 ½ cup chopped apples.

¾ stick of butter.

1 Tbsp flour

1 egg

1 tsp cinnamon

1/8 tsp salt

Put chopped apples in unbaked pie crust. Beat eggs. Add cinnamon, flour, salt, sugar, and margarine. Mix well; pour over chopped apples. Bake at 350 degrees until brown, about 45 minutes.

Better than Anything Cake

By: Amelia Harold

1 box German Chocolate Cake Mix

1 can Eagle brand sweet milk.

1 jar Carmel Syrup

1 tub Cool Whip

1 bag Heath Chips

Fix cake per instructions, once cake cools, poke holes in the top. The more the better. Pour canned milk and caramel on top. Spread cool whip over and top with heath chips. Let the cake sit overnight. The longer it sits the better it gets.

Green Pea Salad

By: Lisa Rogers

1 head of lettuce

1 10oz can green peas

Bacon (as much as you want)

1 chopped or sliced whole onion.

2 cups Shredded Cheddar Cheese

2 cups Mayonnaise

1 tsp sugar

Salt & Pepper

In a 9"x13" pan or a serving bowl, crumble lettuce. Add onion, bacon, ½ the shredded cheese, can of peas, salt and pepper. Mix together. Stir sugar into mayo and pour/spread on top of mixture (if you use miracle whip, do not add sugar). Top with remaining cheese. Serve cold.

Quick Volume Conversions

- 1 tablespoon = 3 teaspoons = 15 milliliters
- 4 tablespoons = 1/4 cup = 60 milliliters
- 1 ounce = 2 tablespoons = 30 milliliters
- 1 cup = 8 oz. = 250 milliliters
- 1 pint = 2 cups = 500 milliliters
- 1 quart = 4 cups = 950 milliliters
- 1 quart = 2 pints = 950 milliliters
- 1 gallon = 4 quarts = 3800 milliliters = 3.8 liters

A Little about the Author

Meagan Lawson is a registered nurse and farmer.

She has mastered cooking from scratch, the easy way, and loves to encourage others to do the same.

She got married in her 20's, her husband always planted a garden. She started learning to cook from scratch and preserve the fresh food.

She found satisfaction in the process and wanted to share it with others.

You can find new recipes and videos on Facebook/YouTube.

True Grit: Southern Cooking and Canning

"No one is born a great cook; one learns by doing."

-Julia Child

A big thank you to everyone that purchased and contributed to this book, it does not go unnoticed, and we hope you enjoyed reading it as much as we enjoyed creating it.

Made in United States
Orlando, FL
15 August 2024

50306243R00042